Walks
on
Bainbridge

By Dave and Alice Shorett

Lakestream Publications

PROCEEDS FROM THIS BOOK WILL BE DONATED TO THE BAINBRIDGE ISLAND LAND TRUST

MAPS
Moore Creative Design, Helena, Montana.

DESIGN
Martha Brouwer, Loft Publishing, Seattle, Washington

PHOTO CREDITS
All photos in this book are the author's except Ron Williamson photos on pages 14, 18, 46, 50, 55, 60.

ISBN 0-9652116-8-1
Published by Lakestream Publications, 200 Maynard Bldg. 119 1st Ave So. Seattle, Wa. 98104 (206)-842-9202

Walks on Bainbridge

By Dave and Alice Shorett

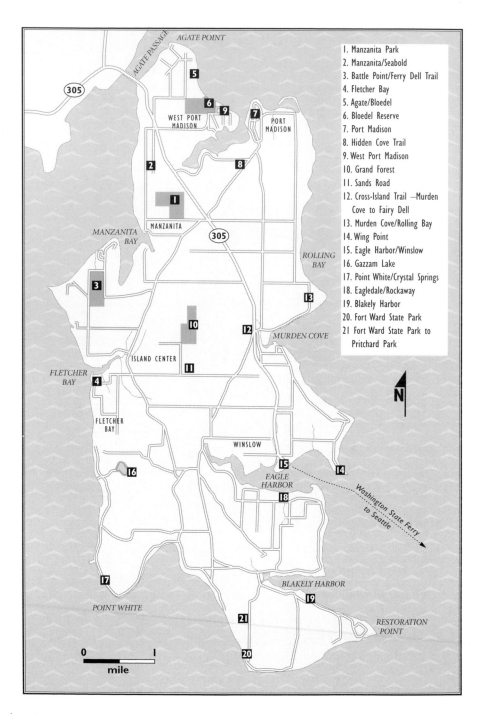

1. Manzanita Park
2. Manzanita/Seabold
3. Battle Point/Ferry Dell Trail
4. Fletcher Bay
5. Agate/Bloedel
6. Bloedel Reserve
7. Port Madison
8. Hidden Cove Trail
9. West Port Madison
10. Grand Forest
11. Sands Road
12. Cross-Island Trail —Murden
    Cove to Fairy Dell
13. Murden Cove/Rolling Bay
14. Wing Point
15. Eagle Harbor/Winslow
16. Gazzam Lake
17. Point White/Crystal Springs
18. Eagledale/Rockaway
19. Blakely Harbor
20. Fort Ward State Park
21. Fort Ward State Park to
    Pritchard Park

Contents

Introduction

A nice walk is surely one of life's great and simple pleasures. When you take that walk on Bainbridge Island, most likely it will be in a beautiful place, among plenty of trees and greenery, with great views of Puget Sound and possibly a visit to the beach.

The Island is blessed with extensive tracts of parkland, numerous bays, some public beaches, and a large number of road ends which allow access to the shoreline. Bainbridge also has a few farms, some semi-rural areas, and many roads bordered by towering trees, old homes, and lovely gardens.

Walking is good for you, both physically and spiritually. We hope those who read this book and take the walks will enjoy the experience, and will also appreciate the beauty of Bainbridge. We also hope some will become active in preserving the natural features of the Island that can be saved from development, or where development does inevitably occur, in taking the initiative to help make that development compatible with the natural state of the land.

The Bainbridge Island Land Trust has been the single most successful force on the Island in preserving land in its natural state. The Grand Forest, Meigs Park and Gazzam Lake Park are all, in our view, preserved primarily due to the efforts of the Land Trust. The Land Trust had help from others, but few would disagree that it was the prime mover in each instance. The Land Trust has saved other land as well and continues to work hard to save more. Whatever profits this book produces will be donated to the Bainbridge Island Land Trust.

USING THIS BOOK
Nearly all walks described in this book are loop walks. A few are out and back walks but for the most part, each attempts to take you on a loop of about 2-3 miles. Most of the walks will take about an hour moving at a steady pace. Included with each described walk are extensions you can take to lengthen your walk.

Bainbridge trail

The book does not attempt to list all of the possible loops on Bainbridge, just the ones which seem most appealing. Some are road walks and others are on paths in parks. The road walks avoid those with heavy traffic. There is light enough vehicular traffic on most Bainbridge roads outside Winslow that they are fine for walking, with very little disturbance except for an occasional car. Drivers are very courteous on the Island, often moving over into the oncoming lane to give you room to walk.

Because Bainbridge continues to be developed, some of what is described will certainly change and no longer be the same as set forth in this book. New roads will appear, some may interrupt trails and some may create nice loops for walking. In 2001, Bainbridge voters passed an 8 million dollar levy to purchase open space. Trails will be developed on some of the land purchased with those funds and additional trails and links will likely be constructed on other land as well. Thus, the maps, which are designed to show the roads and trails as of 2006, will likely become dated and you are advised to ask directions if you become confused when coming upon roads or trails which don't show up on the maps.

Manzanita Park

Basic trail loops, 2-3 miles. Moderate grade. Big time mud and puddles at times.

MANZANITA PARK HAS ALMOST 3 miles of trails crisscrossing its 120 acres. The Bainbridge Saddle Club borders the park on the east and the trails are heavily used by equestrians, so you must be on the lookout for horses. Despite its mixed use, it is a fine place to walk in deep woods. It won't be long before many trees in this park will approach their 100th year. The park accommodates much better walking in dry weather, since it gets muddy and boggy in places in winter. The best time of year is September and October: the trails are driest, the blackberries are abundant and the many deciduous trees

Deep in the Manzanita jungle

have their annual fall display of yellow and red leaves. Small children love to slosh through the mud and puddles during the rainy part of the year. Just figure on having an empty washing machine and a full bathtub ready for the little nippers when they get home.

The entrance to the park is off Day Rd., approximately .4 mile west

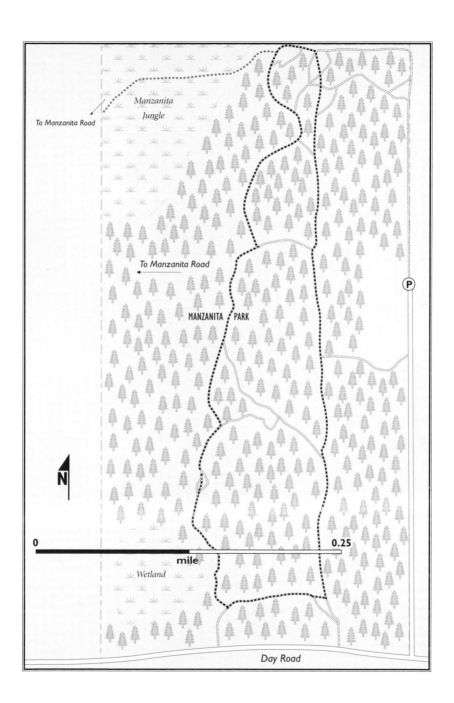

To Manzanita Road

Manzanita Jungle

To Manzanita Road

MANZANITA PARK

P

N

0   0.25

mile

Wetland

Day Road

Manzanita Park Trailhead

of Highway 305. The sign is rather obscure. There is a big parking lot on the left down the entrance road a ways. The formal trail entrance is slightly back toward Day Rd. from the parking area. You can also continue walking past the parking lot area to begin the walk.

Trails go every which way in this park. Take any route you like. The park slopes downhill to the west, and there is some hill climbing to get back to the parking area. If you walk all the trails, you will have gone about 3 miles. At the northeast end, there is a trail heading downhill to what might be called the "Manzanita Jungle." This trail is also accessible from the west side of Manzanita Park from an entry trail off Manzanita Rd., marked by a small sign. A trail and boardwalk once penetrated the jungle and its spruce forest from east and west enabling walkers to cross the park in this direction as well as north-south. The boardwalk was built in the wettest, darkest part of the park and has gradually rotted into the ground in many spots. It won't hold an adult in places and you can fall through. However, in September and October in dry years, before any serious rains begin, you can get through with some effort. At most other times, high rubber boots are necessary and even then, you won't make it

Manzanita Park Trail

in really wet weather. It's actually a bit of an adventure, especially for children. Be sure to stay on the trail. If you are not sure where to go, turn around and head back. This is the thickest of thickets: skunk cabbage, swampy ground, big old mossy trees and bushes, sunlight seldom reaching the ground. If there truly is a bear living on Bainbridge, bet on it living down here somewhere.

Manzanita Road/Seabold

Total road loop distance 3.3 miles. Easy grade. Light traffic.

THIS WALK IS A CLASSIC Bainbridge road walk with access to a park and the beach. Park at the corner of Manzanita and Day roads. For a trip down to the beach before you start the loop, walk south from your car on Manzanita Rd. to the Dock Street road end, an   access popular with kayakers and other small boaters, as hand launching is relatively easy. The road end is just north of the entrance to big and little Manzanita bays, the latter first called "Little Mosquito Bay" and said to have   been   named 'Manzanita' by the first postmistress who mistook the madrona trees (native to the island) for manzanita trees.

Hidden Cove Road End leads to the beach

Back at the car, walk north on Manzanita, renamed Henderson north of its junction with Hidden Cove Road. For another look at the beach, follow Hidden Cove Rd. to its end where there is a sign and the community has built stairs down to the shore. Manzanita/Henderson Road is lined on both sides with 100' tall Douglas fir trees most of the way to Seabold Ave, where it ends. Few property owners have cut the trees next to the road and it is one of the finer roads to walk on Bainbridge. There are some very old homes along the way.

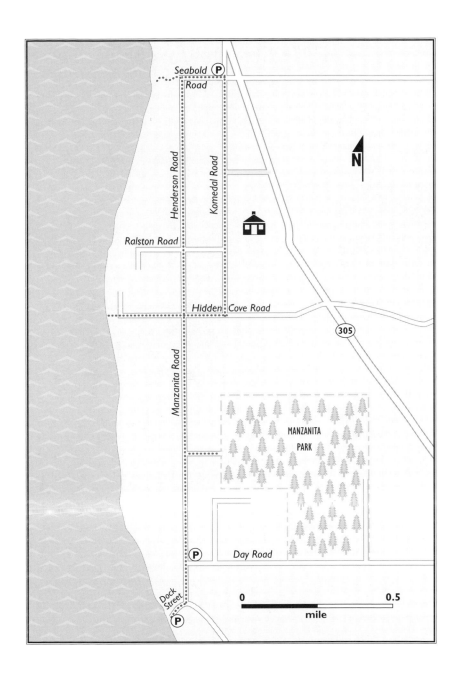

Farmhouse and Olympic Mountains from Komedal Road

As Henderson meets Seabold, there is yet another beach access via a very difficult road end trail west toward the Sound, leading downhill in about 200' to a steep, hazardous path to the beach 75' below. A rope has been tied to trees along this path, a good idea because it is very slippery in wet weather. Exercise extreme caution if attempting to reach the beach.

If you've been down to the beach at the Seabold Rd. end, or skipped it, at the intersection of Seabold and Henderson, turn uphill to Komedal. At the intersection there is a new park built by Bainbridge Rotary Club. Just after you turn south onto Komedal you will see on your right an historic house and farm, with a gabled cupola on its barn, a rectangular heavy timber building typical of the barns once found in the island's agricultural areas.

Travel on Komedal to Hidden Cove Road, passing the Seabold Community Club, a wood frame structure built in 1893 by local residents as the first school in the Seabold community. It was a classic one room schoolhouse. A kitchen was added in 1923 and it was later converted to

Seabold Community Club

a community club. Seabold was apparently the name taken by an early settler who encountered the "bold sea" upon his arrival. It was previously named "Bull Town" after a homesteader, Mr. Bull and was at that time said to be populated entirely by Norwegians. At Hidden Cove Rd., turn west to Manzanita and back to the car.

For an extended walk, one can enter Manzanita Park off Manzanita Rd. about .2 mile north of the corner of Day and Manzanita, where a signed trail leads into the park. There is about .5 mile of trail in this western section of the park. It leads to the west end of the old boardwalk trail through the Manzanita Jungle, passable only in the driest times of year.

Battle Point/Ferry Dell Trail

Basic loop trail inside Battle Point Park 1.5 miles.
Additional loop through Fairy Dell and Arrow Point Dr. adds another 1 mile.

Battle Point Park's popular walking path

BATTLE POINT IS BAIN- BRIDGE'S most frequented park. It is divided about equally between active recreation and open space. It is named for Battle Point, which is not within the park. The point is a nearby peninsula jutting into the Sound, the site of a battle between the Suquamish and northern tribes, which resulted in victory for the Suquamish. The 90-acre park is a former World War II Naval radio transmitter station. It was acquired by the Park District in 1972 and initial development completed in 1980. Most of the park's trees are still quite young and as the years pass, one can see how beautiful this park will become.

The park has a loop trail of 1.5 miles for walkers, bikers, skaters, strollers, and about anything else that moves. It also has a roughly parallel loop equestrian trail, which is fine for walkers as well, set back behind trees and bushes, next to the perimeter fence . There is plenty for kids to do, with a pond full of ducks, bass and bluegill for fishing and an extraordinary kids play area, which attracts folks from all over Kitsap County.

The loop walk can be extended in several ways, the nicest of which is

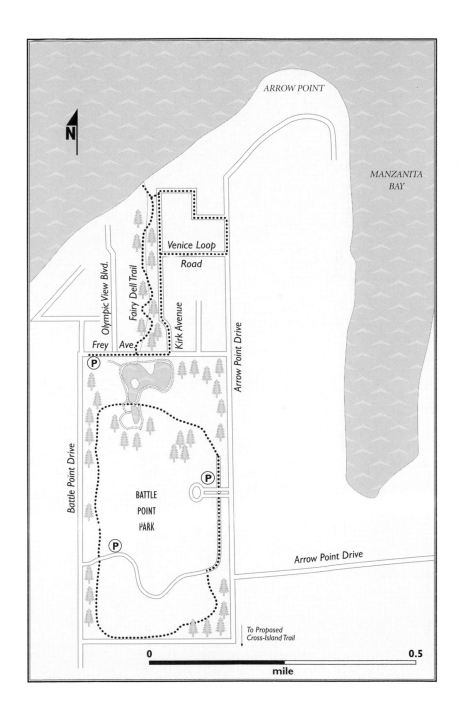

ARROW POINT

MANZANITA
BAY

Venice Loop
Road

Olympic View Blvd.

Fairy Dell Trail

Kirk Avenue

Frey Ave.

Arrow Point Drive

Battle Point Drive

BATTLE
POINT
PARK

Arrow Point Drive

To Proposed
Cross-Island Trail

0   0.5
mile

Fairy Dell Trail

through Fairy Dell Trail. The Fairy Dell trailhead can be seen tucked away in the trees on the north side of the park, along Frey Avenue, just past Olympic View Boulevard. Start down the trail and you are suddenly in a deep forest of fir and cedar. In this natural garden park, church services were held in the open air. Ministers of various Protestant denominations preached in a natural amphitheater from a platform on top of a large stump, while the congregation sat on the banks of the ravine or stood among the trees. The side slopes of Fairy Dell are protected by Kitsap County through a conservation easement. The well maintained trail bends and curves through the ravine, crossing wet areas with bridges. About half way down the trail on your left stands the stump of the once largest living Douglas fir on Puget Sound, the "Bill Taft" tree. Its circumference is thirty feet and it once

Battle Point Pond — home of the giant bluegill

reached 200 feet tall, until a heavy wind took off the top.

Animals in the ravine include chipmunks, squirrels, frogs, tree toads and river otter, which are known to travel this thoroughfare to the pond at Battle Point, where one may sometimes be seen near dark swimming and fishing for bass and bluegill. About 3/4 of the way down the trail, look up on your right at a tall Douglas fir snag where there is an osprey nest. During the summer, you may be able to see an osprey pair raising and feeding a brood of chicks.

The trail soon reaches a mudflat beach where you can spend some time on a sunny day. There is a large colony of sand dollars in the area, so be careful walking in the mud. On your return back up the trail, within a few hundred feet, take a left fork up the well-developed side trail to Kirk Ave and Venice Loop Rd. David Guterson and his family lived at 13024 Venice Loop many years, while he wrote *Snow Falling on Cedars*, a world-wide best selling novel. Head downhill around Kirk Avenue, to Arrow Point Dr., and then back to Battle Point Park's north parking lot area.

Fletcher Bay

Total road loop distance, 2.3 miles. Some uphill grade. Light traffic.

PARK IN THE LOT FOR the stores at the corner of New Brooklyn and Miller Road. Walk west on NE Fletcher Bay Rd. until the road meets NE Foster Rd., along the way crossing a salmon stream, Springbrook Creek. You might get lucky in late fall and see a coho or two heading upstream. The creek was rehabilitated in the 1980's through the combined efforts of landowners, biologists, Eagle Scouts and others. You can get a

Friendly donkey on Hansen Road

look at lovely Fletcher Bay by walking some of the short roads which extend close to the bay by continuing past Foster Rd. and then retracing your steps to continue the loop. There is a public access to the beach at Fletcher Bay off NE Fletcher Bay Landing road end. Foster curves around to meet Hansen Rd. close to the Sound. From here it is uphill with nice views across the narrows to Brownsville and University Point on the Kitsap Peninsula. One can imagine the Ferry Hiyu, later serving the Pt. Defiance to Vashon ferry run, as it sailed between Brownsville and Fletcher Bay up to five times a day beginning in 1924 and continuing for several years.

The entire area is nicely forested. As Hansen heads east to meet Springridge Rd., a pair of donkeys may be out in the field to your left, delighting children and adults alike. Springridge Rd. travels a long downhill route with tall trees on both sides, all the way back to NE Fletcher Bay Rd. and a short uphill to your car. There are several side routes to extend the walk, but none are loops. At the intersection of Hansen and Springridge, a right turn will lead you on Springridge to Gazzam Lake Park.

Several colorful pioneers lived around Fletcher Bay. The bay was once

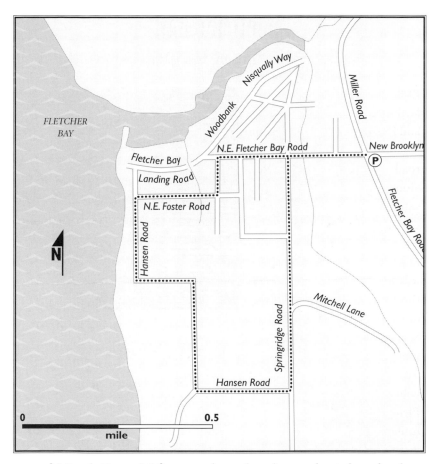

named "Greek George's" for an early settler who was buried on the shore in front of his house. "Logger Olson" homesteaded 160 acres north of the bay. A resort for tourists was built on the bay in 1912, including a pavilion, picnic grounds, a campsite and a store. In 1932, a more elaborate pavilion was built, complete with a bowling alley. Foster Rd. is named for Ma and Pa Foster who built the pavilion. Into the 1950's, Saturday night dancing to the music of Katherine Jacobson and others at the pavilion was a must for many Islanders. Fletcher Bay was also the site of a well-known dairy farm, whose owner won acclaim at the Puyallup Fair for the quality of his dairy milk.

On hot summer days, as the saltwater floods in over the tide flats to reach high tide, Fletcher Bay becomes warm enough for swimming.

Agate/Bloedel

Basic road loop from Dolphin Drive 2.2 miles.
Easy grade, light traffic. Beach access at two points.

THIS IS A NICE, EASY LOOP WALK on roads in the north end of Bainbridge which can be combined with a stroll through 160 acre Bloedel Reserve for a longer excursion. The northern end of Bainbridge still has plenty of tall firs, dark woods, and is reminiscent of the "old Bainbridge."

The road walk begins by turning off Highway 305 at Agatewood Rd. Continue to the intersection with Dolphin Drive and park. Walk down Dolphin Drive to Bloedel Reserve. (See Bloedel Reserve walk) To continue the loop outside Bloedel Reserve, turn left on Agate Point Rd. Walk to North Street, where you can take a side trip about .3 mile to a difficult road end beach access which descends to a good spot to view the shore atop a rock bulkhead. At North Street, turn left and shortly come to a 3-way intersection. One can take a right to the end of Agate St. for an out and back .8 mile addition to the basic loop. The out and back walk down Agate St. takes you closer to the water with some good views toward Suquamish. There is a nice public access to a sandy Agate Pass beach from

Sanwick Road End leads to the beach on Agate Pass

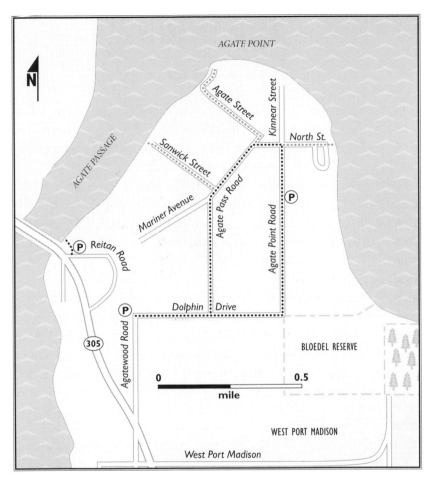

the end of Sanwick St., which you pass off Agate Pass Rd. To complete the walk, follow Agate Pass Rd. back uphill to Dolphin Dr. and back to the car.

There is a nearby drive to waterfront public access on Agate Pass from a small pullout off Reitan Rd., which is reached by turning off Highway 305 just before the Agate Pass Bridge. Follow Reitan until just about under the bridge. Park here and take the path off to the right, leading downhill to the beach. This spot is popular with anglers and beach-combers. In September and October, coho often congregate here on their way to spawn and they can occasionally be seen jumping and milling around. There are 300' of public tidelands extending north of this access.

Bloedel Reserve

Total walk about 2 miles.

THIS WALK WILL COST YOU something, but it is worth it. Just be sure to make a reservation before you visit Bloedel and plan to pay a small fee unless you are a member. (206-842-7631) The primary walk in the Reserve is about 2 miles and takes a couple of hours. Owned by the nonprofit

Pond at Bloedel Reserve

Arbor Fund, established by the Bloedel family, Bloedel Reserve is a world-class botanical reserve which changes dramatically with the seasons. It is worth a visit at least four times a year.

The site of the Reserve was occupied, at least seasonally, by the Suquamish Tribe. An 1827 Hudson Bay Company record states that there was a small village at the mouth of the stream flowing through the site. The now Reserve land was taken by the U.S. government pursuant to the Point Elliot Treaty and passed through a number of owners, including George Meigs, who logged it, and the Collins family, which built a home in the French country style in 1931. The property was eventually purchased by Prentice and Virginia Bloedel in 1951. The Bloedel's wealth came from the family Canadian logging company, with Prentice actively engaged in management. Fortunately for the public, Bloedel, a Yale graduate, had strong views on conservation, especially growing second-growth timber. These views motivated him to create the Reserve. We are the beneficiaries of this man's complex mix of logger/conservationist experience and beliefs.

Without seeming to be, the Reserve is carefully planned and landscaped. Visitors walk slowly through part of its 160 acres, viewing and experiencing forest, meadow, bird marsh, pond, Japanese garden, moss garden, rhododendron glen, and reflection pool environments. It is a good

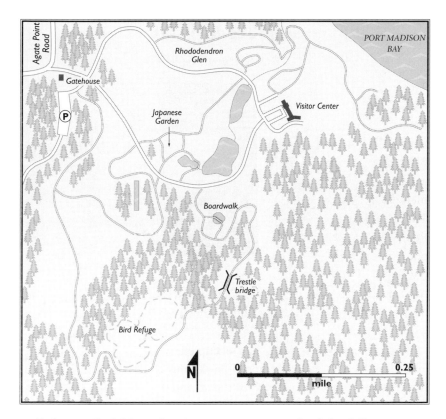

walk for small children, for there is magic in each of the different areas, including bridges and boardwalks, swans and other waterfowl, and plenty of pleasant surprises. The transition from one area to the other is natural and seamless. A visit to the French country house, sited on a bluff overlooking Port Madison Bay and Jefferson Head, is a highlight for most visitors, but the overall experience will leave you awed by the feel of the Reserve. In the words of Prentice Bloedel:

> "Respect for trees and plants replaces indifference; one feels the existence of a divine order . . . One realizes that we humans are trustees in this world, that our power should be exercised in this context. This new awareness determined us to set the land aside for the primary purpose of providing others with the opportunity to enjoy plants both as arranged by man and as they arrange themselves and for the purpose of providing people wandering about the Reserve a refreshing experience of nature and broadening of their appreciation of their world. "

Port Madison

Basic road loop, 2.1 miles. Some moderately steep uphill on W. Euclid.
Extended to Fay Bainbridge State Park, 3.5 miles.
Light traffic except on Phelps Rd. and Hidden Cove Rd.

VISIT HISTORIC PORT MADISON on an easy 2.1 mile walk. Park at the corner of Hidden Cove Road and Phelps Road. Walk north on Phelps to the intersection of Euclid and Washington and from here do the loop in either direction. On W. Euclid walk alongside Port Madison Bay in the sunlight (20% chance in winter, much higher in summer) and get a feel for the historic bay. Visualize the bay filled with black Haida canoes, visitors from the north. Presently, you are likely to see a wide array of watercraft, including some of the many sailboats which moor in the bay. There are a few houses remaining in the Washington and Euclid area which were built around the time of construction of the Port Madison mill. The houses uphill from the water along Washington and Euclid were built in the early 1900's as summer residences after the mill was closed. Note the typical wrap-around verandas and low projecting overhangs with orientation toward Port

Port Madison Bay

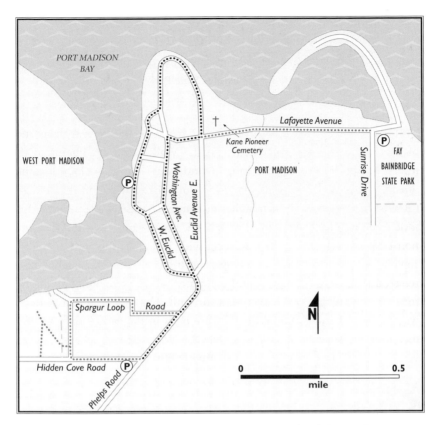

PORT MADISON
BAY

WEST PORT MADISON

Lafayette Avenue

Kane Pioneer
Cemetery

PORT MADISON

FAY
BAINBRIDGE
STATE PARK

Sunrise Drive

Washington Ave.

Euclid Avenue E.

W. Euclid

Spargur Loop   Road

Hidden Cove Road

Phelps Road

N

0   0.5
mile

Madison Bay. There are blackberries on the shore side of the road in season and it is a good place to pick them. There is a public road end at the end of Lafayette allowing access to the shoreline. It is marked with an historical interpretative sign. Don't let the "Port Madison Private Property" signs on either side keep you from walking down the path.

The walk can be extended from the E. Euclid part of the loop by following Lafayette east .3 mile to historic Kane Cemetery, founded in 1860, where some notable Island pioneers are buried. From the back of the cemetery there is an unusual view to the east of the Bainbridge "sandspit." Across the road is a heron rookery reported to have as many as 110 nests. You can see the large nests high up in the trees from the edge of the road. Continue on Lafayette up a fairly steep hill and down to the end of the road, where there is an entrance to Fay Bainbridge State Park. Here, you can either take a walk out the Sand Spit, on a road between beachfront

Port Madison Historic Home

homes on both sides, or enter the park. The park is sited upon the land that was the home and farm of the Fay family. It is reported that John Fay, a lawyer, conveyed it to the State to be a park, conditioned upon it carrying the family name. (If all lawyers presently on Bainbridge followed suit, half the island's waterfront would become park.) The park is 17 acres with 1400' of public beach, picnic facilities, camping and other amenities. It has a boat launch suitable for kayaks and small sailboats and the sandy beach is a favorite for children and even a swimmer or two in hot weather.

There is yet another little loop to keep you walking, through Spargur Loop to Hidden Cove Rd., and then back to the car, passing pastureland, tiny T'Chookwap Park, the Seattle Yacht Club and the entrance to a fine new waterfront park along the way. This park was purchased with Open Space Bonds in 2005. It is presently accessible from just downhill of the intersection of Hidden Cove Rd. and Spargur Loop. The park is approximately 5 acres, with a lovely meadow, tall old trees and a nice dock. Plans for the park include use of the dock by those using kayaks, canoes, sailboats and any other human-powered water-craft.

This sheltered bay was given various names through its history. It was called "Tchoak-um-cguck"(or "Tkouchook-wap"), "crawling up in there," by the Suquamish, who had a village site on the bay. The name apparently refers to the way inner Port Madison Bay winds narrowly inland a long distance. On May 10, 1841, officers in the

Frog Rock — A Bainbridge landmark

Wilkes expedition surveyed the outer bay and named it "Port Madison," after President James Madison.

The Port Madison Mill Company, partly owned by George A. Meigs, operated in the harbor from 1854 to 1892. Port Madison was a full-fledged town with a general store, machine shop, a brass and iron foundry, wharf, warehouse and a hotel. There were more than 300 people living and working in Port Madison during its busiest years as a mill town. When Kitsap County was formed in January 1857, the county seat was located at Port Madison, As the county seat, Port Madison had a courthouse, at Luclid and Washington, jail, school and lending library. The Port Madison Mill closed in 1892 and the next year the county seat was moved.

Chief Sealth visited Mr. Meigs of the Port Madison mill frequently. He spent his last years with his people at the Suquamish Reservation and at Agate Point on Bainbridge Island in a house near his granddaughter Mary. Chief Sealth died in 1866. If you drive to Suquamish, you can visit his burial site in the Suquamish Cemetery, overlooking the entrance to Agate Pass, and the site of the Old Man House on the shore of the pass. Both are among the most significant sites on Puget Sound.

Hidden Cove Trail

2.5-3 mile trail out and back with small interior loops, through forest on a well-graded path. Moderately steep in a few spots. Planned access to a waterfront park.

ONE OF THE CONDITIONS required of the Hidden Cove development resulted in construction of a nice trail meandering through woods approximately 3 miles, when all the loops are taken. This trail is a very good example of what can be done when trails are mandated as a condition for development of a substantial area. While we know that not all undeveloped land can be kept intact in a natural state, if large tracts are to be developed, trails such as this one make the development a lot more palatable to walkers and nature lovers.

Hidden Cove Trail

The trail begins at the northwest corner of the Hidden Cove ball field, at the wooded edge of left field on the northern diamond. Look for a small trail sign. Generally, there is plenty of parking available in the lot. The trail heads off through the woods, passing a few houses on the right, then parallels Hidden Cove Road for a distance. A newly purchased waterfront park lies west across Hidden Cove Rd. Eventually signs and a path will lead walkers across Hidden Cove Rd. to the park. Once beyond this point much of the trail is out of sight of houses and roads. It has a variety of grades, with some uphill and downhill, enough to get you breathing hard if you are traveling fast. The trail is popular with joggers as well as walkers.

The trail eventually crosses a creek and heads uphill, winding around

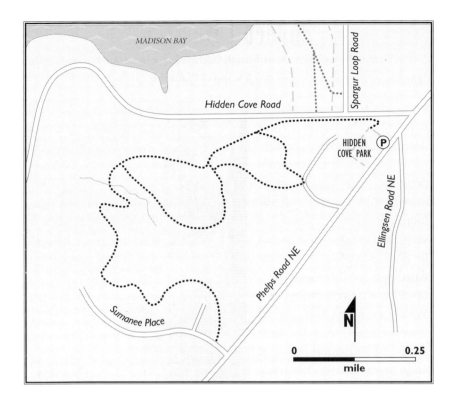

until it comes out on Sumanee Place N.E. road. By this point, you have walked better than one mile. Turn around here and head back, taking the first major right. This side trail will take you up to a road and holding pond. Directly across the road, the trail continues and eventually intersects with the main trail. There is another small loop side trail heading off to the right on the main trail along the way back.

The Hidden Cove trail takes a little over an hour to walk in its entirety. The surrounding forest is notable for the number of cedar trees and huge cedar stumps remaining from the old logging days, some with springboard notches. One can find wild blackberries early in summer and huckleberries later. The trail has moss covered trees and snags, giving a bright green hue to much of the walk. It is a nice place to walk in the rain and in the dark days of winter. The trail is well constructed and drains effectively. The walk may be a bit too strenuous for small children to cover the entire loop but it can be a nice aerobic walk for anyone else.

West Port Madison

A basic road walk of about one mile round trip. Three road end beach access points.
Extensions, Grottle .5, Skogen .5 and Sivertson 1.0. Light traffic, moderate grade.

FROM HIGHWAY 305, turn off to West Port Madison/NE County Park Rd. Park at West Port Madison Park or drive on to Broom St. where there is good parking just around the corner and near the road end. West Port Madison Park is a 23-acre nature preserve which has the feel of a venerable old forest, as some of its trees are well over 100 years old. It was the first public park on Bainbridge Island. Across the bay are Indianola and Jefferson Head, popular fishing spots. Unfortunately, it is impossible to reach the beach from the park. Beach access is available at the undeveloped and somewhat difficult to find public road end off Gordon NE, which is used as a neighborhood access point. If using this access, respect the rights of those who maintain it for neighborhood use and don't disturb their boats.

Walking downhill from West Port Madison Park, NE County Park Rd. bends to become Broom St. and leads to a very nice road end public access to the beach. It is approximately .5 mile from the park. Just upland of the beach there is a 1932 Daughters of the American Revolution plaque affixed

West Port Madison Park picnic shelter

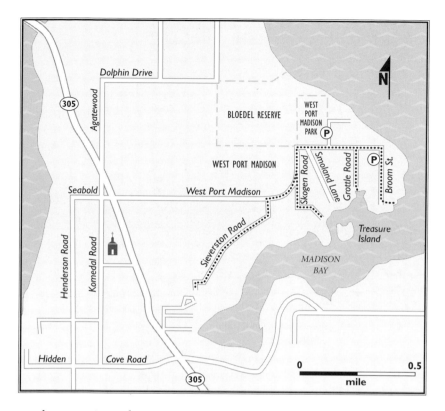

to a large granite rock, commemorating an 1861 Independence Day celebration held at that spot. The rock is said to have been brought from British Columbia to Bainbridge by the last ice age's continental glacier 10,000 years ago. It was taken by truck to this spot, connecting the past to the present. The 1861 celebration is said to be the first "Grand Old Fourth of July" event on the island, a predecessor to the annual affair held in Winslow. This scenic spot was called "The Maples" and some of the same maple trees still stand at the site. The public beach is about 50' wide and in the heat of the summer, one will find swimmers here.

On your way back, for an extended walk, take Grottle Rd. .2 mile to a secluded grassy road end, particularly nice at high tide but basically a mudflat when the tide is out; Skogen .4 mile to a great road end with views across the bay to Treasure Island and the new park on Spargur Loop; or walk Sivertson Rd. .5 mile to its end, along a very shady winding road with virtually no traffic.

Grand Forest

Loop through West and East sections, 4 miles.

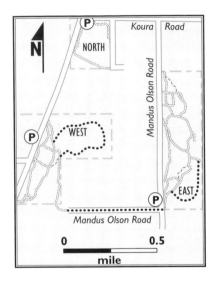

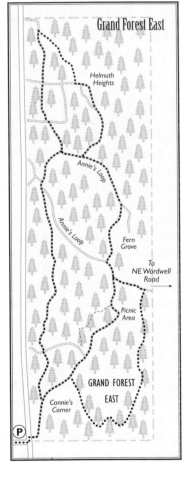

THROUGH AN INTENSE CITIZEN EFFORT, led by the Bainbridge Island Land Trust, the 240-acre Grand Forest Park was purchased in 1991 from Washington's Department of Natural Resources. The park is primarily second growth forest. For the statistically minded, there are an estimated 54,000 trees in the Grand Forest. It is large enough that it provides habitat to a variety of animals, including deer, squirrel, rabbit, raccoon, red fox, and resident and migratory birds. Quiet, careful observation will bring some surprising sightings.

The park is divided into three parts: Grand Forest North, West and East. There are approximately 5 miles of trail, nearly all of which are in the West and East portions. All have trails through second-growth forest, wetlands and wildlife habitat. The West and East sections have much

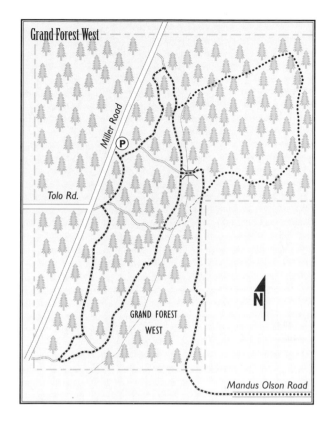

longer trails and it is not difficult to walk both by using Mandus Rd, which connects the two. There are ongoing attempts to connect all three by trail. Forty acres in the northwest section of the East portion is owned by the Bainbridge School District and may be developed as a school site, unless other arrangements can be made.

Before the Grand Forest became a park, it was commonly used by walkers, bikers and equestrians and there is a confusing web of trails, particularly in the East section. A one mile trail addition, rapidly becoming a favorite route, has been built on the southeast portion of the East section. The signs in the East section allow one to take a variety of routes on a loop.

The East section is more open forest and has great huckleberries in season. You may also encounter a mushroom picker or two during mushroom season. The outside loop in this section is just over 2 miles and can be traveled easily by most small children. During monsoon time, there are

Grand Forest bridge

some great muddy stretches and major puddles, just right for little kids with rubber boots. There is some up and down terrain, but for the most part it is quite level.

The West section trail crosses Issei Creek and has a deep forest feel as it winds through trees and over grades. There are some very old trees in this section, you can easily feel you are in an Olympic forest, while still a long way from Olympic National Park. This part of the Grand Forest is well known for its abundant trillium bloom, generally at its peak around Mother's Day.

Probably the best way to walk the Grand Forest is to park at the entrance to the East section on Mandus Olson Rd., walk it in a loop and make your way to the West section downhill via Mandus Olson Rd., which connects the two on the south border of each. Walk west, straight down the gravel drive-way to reconnect with the trail. After walking the West section, return on Mandus Olson Rd. to your car. The route can be reversed by parking in the Grand Forest parking lot on Miller Rd. The loop will give you at least 4 miles in some very fine forest. The Grand Forest can also be entered from Wardwell Rd. by parking on the east end of Wardwell, walking west up Wardwell, then on McRedmond Lane trail on into the park.

If you want to walk the north section of the Grand Forest, park on Koura Rd. just off Miller Rd. The trail begins right there. Unfortunately, the north and south Grand Forest sections are not contiguous and cannot be reached except by a long trudge alongside heavy traffic on Miller Rd.

Grand Forest trail

Sands Road

2.4 miles out and back. Very flat, light traffic.

THIS WALK IS A SIMPLE OUT AND BACK, leisurely, easy walk. Sands Road is flat, passing through a residential area, a school site, and wetlands until it heads uphill at Paulanna Lane and forks into two private roads. There is very little traffic and it is a pleasant inland walk. At the forks, a wetland valley is below to the north, a reminder of how much of the island fortunately remains undevelopable.

Paulanna Lane

Park at the corner of High School Road and Sands Road and head north. At one time, the northwest corner of this intersection was a tree farm. A large tract of land is fenced off to the left, hopefully to stay in its undeveloped state for some time to come. North of the end of the fence begins a school site. Just before Sands' intersection with New Brooklyn, head a short distance up Walden to see one of the oldest log cabins on Bainbridge. There are few left and this is fine specimen.

Cross New Brooklyn and contin-

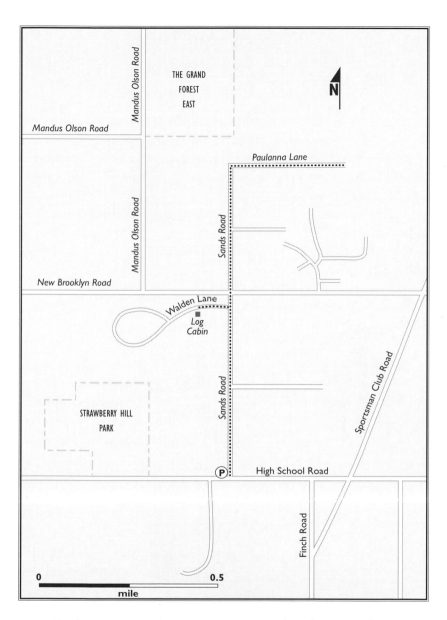

ue to Paulanna Lane.   Once you gain some altitude, you will pass the remnants of an old farm to the left and eventually, a nearly pristine valley. At this juncture, you must turn around and walk back.

Cross Island Trail

Murden Cove to Fairy Dell

Trail with some road crossings, approximately 5 miles one way

ONE OF THE OLDEST DREAMS of many walkers on Bainbridge Island has been a cross-island trail, connecting the beaches on the west side and east side. The Open Space Commission purchased a link between the Grand Forest and Battle Point Park in 2004 and the cross-island route became a reality. We describe it as a "route" rather than a trail, because it requires some road walking, crossing a busy road and a highway, and has one short out and back section. Nevertheless, this approximately 5 mile walk will allow a long one-way trek and the experience of visiting both east and west sides of the island on the same trip.

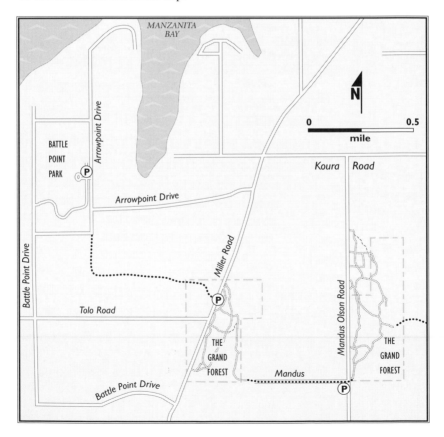

The best way to do this walk is to arrange to be picked up or leave a vehicle at both ends. On the east side, park at Murden Cove (see Murden Cove walk) if you can find parking. Otherwise, leave a vehicle at the east end of Wardwell Rd. The other vehicle can be left in the north parking lot of Battle Point Park. Less confusion will arise if you travel from east to west, beginning at Murden Cove or Wardwell Rd.

If you start at Murden Cove, it is necessary to walk up Manitou Beach Rd. on a narrow shoulder, cross SR 305, and proceed straight ahead west to Wardwell Rd. This is a bit intimidating and certainly noisy for those seeking a quiet walk. You may choose to park and start at Wardwell instead.

From the east end of Wardwell Rd., walk west. Wardwell is a quiet, scenic road. Be sure to visit the goats near the east end of the road. They

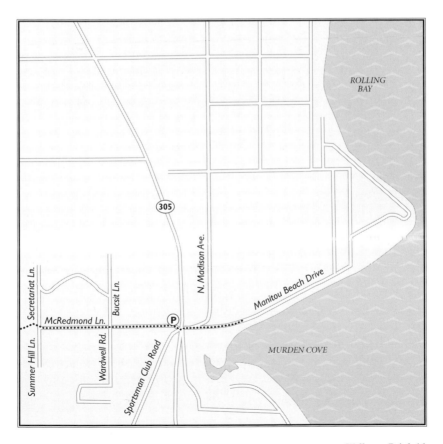

Wardwell Road goat looking for handouts

are friendly and unabashed con artists, in search of food. At one time, the owner provided food in a jar and a donation box. Stay on Wardwell until you reach the intersection with McRedmond Ln, a gravel road. At this point a trail abuts the gravel road on its north side, continues west and eventually enters the Grand Forest, passing under a power line along the way, and traveling up a fairly steep slope into the Grand Forest. When you reach the power line, head right, then uphill into the Grand Forest.

Until a different link between the eastern and western Grand Forest sections is developed, follow the instructions in the Grand Forest section of this book to reach the western Grand Forest parking lot. Directly across Miller Rd. from the lot is the entry to the next link, expected to be built in 2006, traveling approximately one mile through old forest west to exit the trees onto a small road. This road travels north/south. Turn

McRedmond Lane leads to the Grand Forest

right and walk to Battle Point Park, where there will be an entrance to the park through the park's fence. You will find yourself in the southeast corner of the park, near the pea patches and a horse arena.

Once in Battle Point Park, follow the walk directions in the Battle Point Park section of this book to complete the walk.

Murden Cove/Rolling Bay

Basic loop, 2.3 miles, moderate traffic. To Rolling Bay and back, another 1 mile.

PARKING IS LIMITED ON MANITOU BEACH DR. and Murden Cove Dr. E. but parking and beginning at the bottom of Manitou Beach Dr. after it comes off Highway 305 and over the hill down to Murden Cove makes this a nicer walk. Alternatively, park just off Highway 305 on the west side of Moran where it intersects Manitou Beach Dr. and carefully walk downhill on Manitou Beach Dr., or park at the Jiffy Mart on Valley Rd. and walk the route in reverse.

As you walk along the road with Murden Cove to the southeast, there is a great view of Seattle and seabirds to watch. Look for signs marking a 200' stretch of public beach. Native Americans are said to have "swarmed" the bay at times, harvesting shellfish and fishing seasonally. The road was shored up through a WPA project in 1938 which installed 680' of log bulkhead. You pass the site of the Falk homestead, the first in this part of Bainbridge. Walk uphill, taking the curve. At the intersection with Manitou Park Boulevard you can take a side trip to Rolling Bay or

Seattle view from Murden Cove tideflat

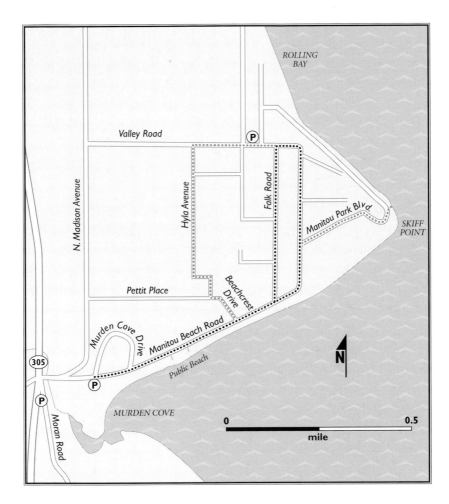

continue straight on.

If you walk down Manitou Park Boulevard, you will see on your left a number of old buildings and a stucco Italian Renaissance style complex dating from 1915, originally developed as the site of the Chautauqua Resort Hotel. It was converted by Frank Moran into a boys school until 1938, then used as the Puget Sound Naval Academy until 1952 when the buildings were purchased for use as a senior residential center. The four-story Moran School Auditorium has a two-story theater complete with stage.

The walk along Manitou Park Blvd. NE ends downhill at a small road end access to the beach on Rolling Bay. When hop growing was thriving in the Duwamish Valley, tribes came from as far as Canada to harvest hops, using Skiff Point as one of their stopping points. Walk back the same way you came and you've added about a mile to the loop, or walk several miles on the beach at a very low tide, all the way to Fay Bainbridge State Park. This is one of Bainbridge's great beach walks, but you must watch the tides carefully.

If you pass up Rolling Bay, continue past Manitou Park Blvd. NE and on uphill to the curve in Manitou as it becomes Valley. At the bend is one of the most stupendous views on Bainbridge, north past Possession Point and Whidbey Island to Mt. Baker and the tall buildings of Vancouver (use your imagination) and direct-

Rolling Bay beach

ly across and south to Shilshole, Seattle and Elliot Bay. Where Valley Rd. meets Falk Rd., you can either turn down Falk and walk downhill along another great Bainbridge road with 100' firs on both sides (for the time being - we hope they are saved from development) back to Murden Cove Dr. E., turn right and stroll back to the car or continue on Valley Rd. to Hyla Ave and follow it as it winds back down to Murden Cove Dr. E.

Murden Cove is fed by the Island's largest creek, Manitou Creek, a healthy salmon and cutthroat stream, flowing from the Meigs Park wetlands, the island's "central valley." Murden Cove supports a large variety of waterfowl, including flocks of goldeneye, grebes, surf scoters, buffleheads, cormorants and many others. Red wing blackbirds sing out from the cattails of the marsh lands inland from the road, and eagles and osprey can sometimes be seen overhead.

Murden Cove

Wing Point

Basic road loop via Byron, 2.75 miles, moderate traffic.
Includes a side trip to a sandy beach on Eagle Harbor

THERE ARE ALL KINDS OF LOOP walks possible in the Wing Point area, as well as one very nice beach access to Eagle Harbor. This is a good walk for visitors arriving on the ferry. One can start from the ferry parking lot or from a parking spot. Parking possibilities are Wing Point Way on the right side across from Azalea Ave., next to the trailhead down to the shoreline, Azalea itself, or you can park in or near the small park at the corner of Grand and Aaron and reverse the walk.

From Ferncliff, walk down Wing Point Way on the left shoulder, pass over Hawley Creek, once said to support

Sandy beach and cattail marsh on Eagle Harbor

spawning salmon but now degraded by development. The mouth of the creek was the site of a Native American fish camp. Continue uphill, looking for a trailhead sign on the right side of the road. The trail leads downhill through heavy forest to 660' of sandy public beach. Locally named the Hall Property, this 11 acre park was purchased with open space bonds. It is a great place to take kids - they love the short walk and the beach. Ferries pass by and there is an excellent view of Mt. Rainier and Joel Pritchard Park. There is an extensive marsh, home to a variety of birds, particularly red wing blackbirds which love to sing in the spring and summer.

Once you return from the Hall Property to Wing Point Way, continue uphill, literally between holes of the Wing Point Golf Club. This is one of the oldest courses in the Northwest, with the clubhouse built in 1916 and

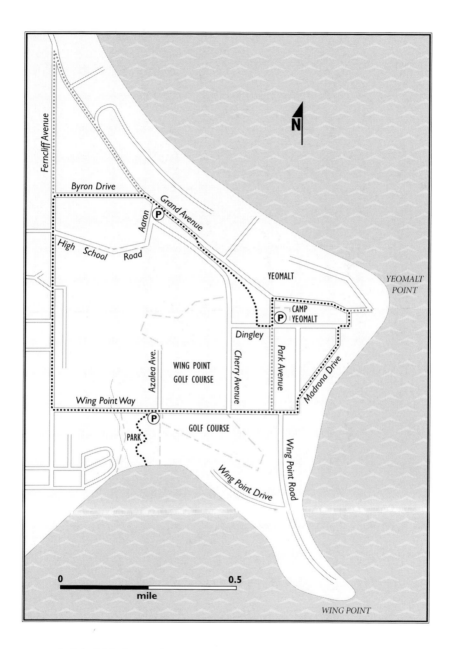

expanded to 18 holes in the 1990's.   Continue on to Fairview, admire the
view of Seattle through the trees and houses, head left and onto Madrona
Dr. When it meets Yeomalt Pt. Dr., you can either continue the loop by

Camp Yeomalt

heading left, or take a side trip downhill sharply for another great view then back uphill. Yeomalt Pt., a Suquamish tribal campsite, was once known as Dead-Man's Bar, in "honor" of a corpse which floated in one day. The Yeomalt area was also the site of the "Yeomalt Club," established in 1910, later the "Yeomalt Lodge" and even later a roller rink. A YWCA camp once occupied 18 acres north of the point. There is presently no public access to the beach.

Where Yeomalt Point Dr. meets Grand Ave, turn left on Park Ave, visit historic Camp Yeomalt on your left, continue to Dingley, turn right, and turn right again onto what is called the Wing Point Nature Trail. Follow it to its intersection with Cherry Ave and walk north briefly on Grand Ave to Byron. A left here takes you back to Ferncliff and south to the starting point for walkers coming from the ferry.

Wing Point neighborhood

Eagle Harbor/Winslow

Loop Walk 1.75 miles, moderate to heavy traffic.
Sunday Cove road end and trail, add .6 mile

THIS WALK TAKES YOU THROUGH the town center of Winslow and along the Eagle Harbor waterfront, providing four points for public access to the shoreline and views of an interesting harbor filled with boats and waterfowl. Eagle Harbor extends inland about 1.5 miles, and the last .5 mile is mudflat and marsh. It is said to be named by the Suquamish and Wilkes Expedition for the common sighting of eagles soaring above the water. Eagle Harbor is used by the Washington State Ferries, private marinas and yacht clubs, boats anchored and moored mid-harbor, sailing clubs, kayakers, rowers, water skiers and lots of waterfowl. Historically, the Winslow harbor had a very active shipyard and marine railway from 1903 to 1960, producing 22

Waterfront trail boardwalk

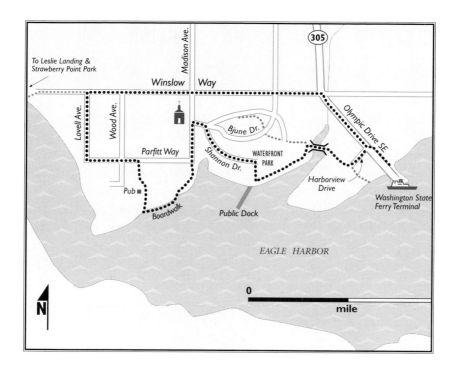

WWII U.S. Navy built mine sweepers and many other vessels.

From the ferry terminal at Winslow, cross the auto lanes at the crosswalk uphill from the terminal and take Harborview Dr. toward the Eagle Harbor Condominiums. (For an immediate side trip, you can turn here toward the waterfront on your left and take a public access path to a no-bank beach and tide flats.) Turn right off Harborview Dr. along a gravel path next to the Washington State Ferries boat yard and cross a small bridge over the ravine and "Winslow Ravine Creek." Here you are on a path in Winslow Waterfront Park. Turn left on the trail toward the water through salal and madrona trees, continue along the trail next to the water. At low tide kids can enjoy the beach at Waterfront Park. The path follows the shoreline of the park toward a public dock where you can walk out to the end and watch boat traffic or, during summer, rent a kayak, canoe or even a pedal-powered swan boat. Long ago, children rowed or canoed across from the opposite shore of Eagle Harbor to attend school. The dinghies lined up on the dock are used primarily by adults and kids

Winslow's Waterfront Park trail

living on boats in the harbor, as well as a few people, mainly ferry commuters, who still row or motor across from the south side.

Back on shore, continue along the waterfront and up to the pavement to Shannon Drive, passing by the small community of condominiums and residences. Walk on the street up to Bjune where you turn left and walk until you are facing historic Eagle Harbor Congregational Church, the first church built on Bainbridge. The bell in the tower was "stolen" in 1974 and discovered more than a year later in a wooded area near the Agate Pass bridge.

Turn left toward the water at Madison Avenue South, follow it to the shore and through Winslow Wharf Marina until you reach a boardwalk over the water. Take the boardwalk to a pub and slightly beyond if you wish. There are benches where you can bring your lunch or just rest and watch heron and ducks. When the grebes and other "bait birds" are in, they can be seen diving and swimming under water - their speed will amaze you. Walk up a set of stairs at Stetson Place, next to the pub, through the pub parking lot to Parfitt Street, then left along the street.

Leslie Landing

Pass through a residence-lined street downhill to Lovell. If you want to visit the shoreline, turn left on Lovell and go to the end of the paved road. There is a locking bar gate and post, and the access offers a view of Hornbeck Spit and inner Eagle Harbor.

To continue on the main route, walk up Lovell to the intersection with Winslow Way, where there is another inviting side trip. A left turn downhill to Sunday Cove affords yet another public access to the shoreline. The paved road leads to the water and a path to the right along the shore for a short distance at Leslie Landing. Eventually, the trail along Leslie Landing will lead to a waterfront park at the site of an old strawberry packing plant. Take this side trip for another view of the harbor or follow the street back up Winslow Way along the sidewalk to visit Winslow shops, movie theaters, and the Farmer's Market. At the intersection of Winslow Way and Highway 305, turn right and return to the ferry terminal.

Gazzam Lake

Basic internal trail loop 2.5 miles.
Close Addition adds 1.6 mile, out and back.
Peters Tree Farm Addtion adds loop of 1.8 mile.
Gazzam Lake Park from Marshall Rd. entrance to
Schell-Scheb Estuary on Rich Passage, 3.0 miles.

441 ACRE GAZZAM LAKE PARK IS LOCATED on the southwest quadrant of the island. The initial footprint of Gazzam Lake Park contained 318 acres of forests and wetlands with Gazzam Lake as the focal point, thirteen and a half acres of pond and marsh. In 1995 the park was purchased through a publicly voted bond combined with grants. There is a conservation easement on the forest land, wildlife habitat, wetlands, and watershed. Because the park is a wildlife sanctuary, there is no swimming or fishing in the lake.

Gazzam Lake Park has mature second growth conifer forests, with stands of Douglas fir, western hemlock, and western red cedar. You can also see western white pine, madrona, big leaf maple, and Pacific yew. Snags within the forest are home to birds such as northern pygmy owls, great horned owls, brown creepers, and various woodpeckers. On a good day, one may spot pileated woodpeckers in snags and Chinese pheasants in bushes next to the trail.

Gazzam Lake may have been formed by glacial activity, which left a large ice chunk within a depression. There is an ancient topographic outlet flowing to the southwest. The shallow lake obtains its water from precipitation, and surface water from the adjoining area. In summer the lake is classified as a "palustrine" or freshwater wetland, a shallow open water pond, which becomes vegetated with yellow pond lily. The pond lily dies back in winter, exposing the open water. Islanders were able to ice skate on the lake in the cold winters of the 1930's and 40's. A variety of waterfowl frequent the lake, including some exotic ducks.

There is access to the shore of the lake in two or three places, where you can sit and watch birds come and go. By design there are no trails around the north and east sides of the lake. A portion of the park is protected from human intrusion, leaving the resident wildlife a place completely their own.

The lake is named after W. L. Gazzam, an early settler and landown-

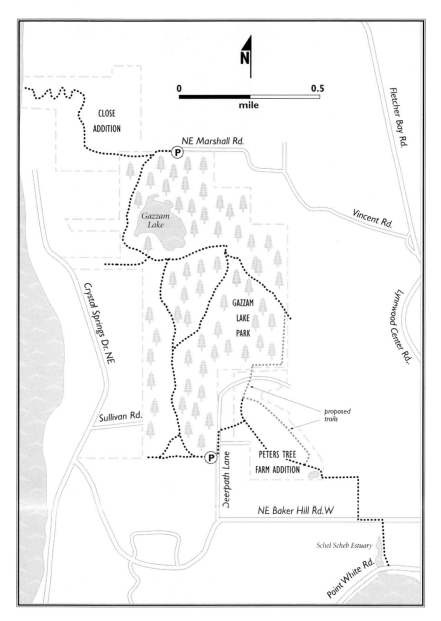

er in this part of the island. The Gazzam House, constructed in 1915, is built of stone with a great rock fireplace and still stands on the shore of Puget Sound at Crystal Springs to the west of the park.

Enter the park off Marshall Rd. or Deerpath Rd. Both entrances lead

Schel Scheb Estuary

shortly to the main trail, which allows a nice loop in the southern half
and a heavily wooded trail curving around about half of Gazzam Lake in
the northwest section.

Close Addition to Gazzam Lake Park

IN 2005, OPEN SPACE BOND FUNDS in partnership with Bainbridge Land
Trust fund raising, facilitated the purchase of a 64 acre addition to Gazzam
Lake Park. The addition is locally described as the "Close Property." To
walk this property, take the Marshall Rd. entrance to a fork, and travel
straight ahead. (It is likely that Springridge Rd. will be extended south
across this trail, requiring walkers to cross it in future years.) The old road
bed/trail heads over a ridge and steadily downhill about .5 mile, leading
to a sign directing walkers to the right. From this point, the trail switch-
backs steeply through deep forest all the way down to 550' of beach accessible only by this trail or by boat. The boundaries of the publicly owned
shoreline are marked and visitors are asked to stay on the public beach.

The total length of the Close Property trail is approximately .8 mile.
This trail allows visitors to Gazzam Lake Park to visit both the lake and the

western waterfront of Bainbridge in the same trip. A trail extension allowing a loop walk in the Close addition is planned for construction in 2006.

Peters Addition to Gazzam Lake Park

THE PETERS TREE FARM IS A 49 ACRE addition to Gazzam Lake Park, lying south and east. Through the assistance of Olemara Peters, Open Space Funds were utilized to purchase this land. Like the Close addition, it is in essentially pristine condition. Soon after purchase, the Park District, with volunteer assistance, constructed a trail which takes walkers downhill approximately .7 mile to a small pond in a very quiet and lovely spot. Bicycle and horse travel on this trail are prohibited and the dam at the south end of the pond is off-limits. The trail skirts the pond on the east side, eventually exiting the Peters addition, where it intersects a presently unpaved public right of way. This right of way, eventually likely to be a roadway, leads south to Baker Hill Rd.

At the north end of the pond, a trail will be built, heading up through a ravine, one of the finest forest settings on Bainbridge, to connect back with the existing side of the loop. The ravine trail will have extraordinary environmental restrictions on its use - walkers only, no horses or bicycles, no cell phones, to name a few - to maintain the relatively undisturbed ecology of the land in the ravine.

The addition of the Close Property and Peters Tree Farm to Gazzam Lake Park will allow a long walk almost entirely in the forest, with the necessity of crossing possibly two roads.

With open space funds, the City of Bainbridge has also acquired a parcel and trail easement on the Schel-Scheb estuary, and 300' of public beach along Point White Drive. This acquisition enables walkers and others to visit the west shore of the Island at the Close addition, walk through the main trails of Gazzam Lake Park, down through the Peters addition, out the public right of way to Baker Hill Road, to Schel-Scheb Creek, and south on the Schel-Scheb public land to the Schel-Scheb estuary on Rich Passage. This trip can be taken one way or as a loop by leaving a vehicle at either end. The grade is downhill most of the way from the Marshall Rd. entrance. The total distance one way from Marshall Rd. is estimated to be three miles.

Point White/Crystal Springs

To Baker Hill Rd. intersection and return, 2.8 miles.
To road end and back, 5.4 miles. Moderate grade, moderate traffic.
Loop up and over Baker Hill, steep grade, moderate to heavy traffic, 4.8 miles.

THIS WALK IS YOUR BEST BET for an afternoon stroll in the sunshine on Bainbridge. Any time of the year when the sun is shining, you can plan on finding the bright light here. In winter, this walk is a temporary cure for the Northwest's most common ailment, Seasonal Affective Disorder. Park on the water side shoulder just around the curve to the west of Point White or at the Point White Dock, which will make this walk considerably shorter. Walk along Crystal Springs Road in the sunshine, observing birds on the water side and the homes on the land side of the road, some of which remain summer homes. Crystal Springs was probably named for the abundance of clear flowing springs along the hillside in this neighborhood. Bremerton and Port Orchard lie far down the inlet to the southwest and Illahee is directly across once you are about 1/4 the way along Crystal Springs Road.

For many years, there has been discussion about a bridge to the Bremerton side from this area. Island residents have always successfully resisted this proposal and if you take this walk you will understand why.

There are few places where you can walk any closer to Puget Sound without actually walking the beach. A 1935 WPA project constructed

Crystal Springs area from Pt. White dock

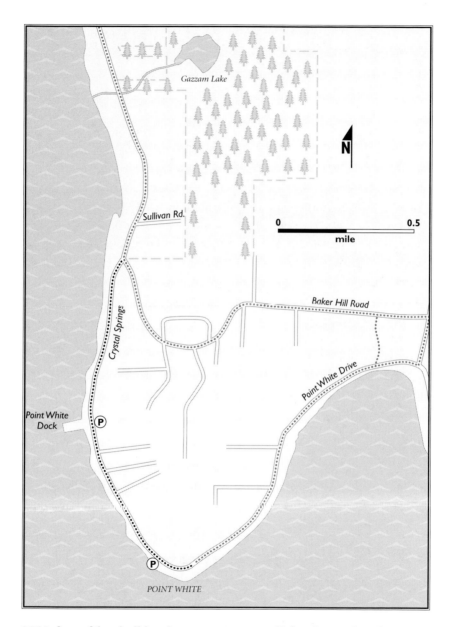

Gazzam Lake

N

Sullivan Rd.

0   0.5
mile

Baker Hill Road

Crystal Springs

Point White Drive

Point White
Dock

(P)

(P)

POINT WHITE

3000 feet of log bulkhead as a retaining wall for the road. The Point
White Dock is open to the public and extends into deep enough water for
anglers and crabbers. At certain times of year, salmon and sea-run cutthroat pass along the shoreline here. Historically, there have been perch

Pt. White dock

and other bottom fish nearby. North of the dock offshore from a gazebo are pilings, all that remains of Gibson Landing, where steamers landed throughout the mid 30's. Across the street is the Munro house/store. On a summer afternoon you may encounter members of the Munro family on the beach next to a gazebo, including Ralph Munro, who for many years was Washington's Secretary of State.

Continue on the road past the Point White dock through the bucolic beach community, a remnant of "old Bainbridge." Just north of the last home on the right before the road begins to climb, there are 7.4 acres of new park land donated to the City and Park District by Joyce and David Veterane. The donation includes 550' of waterfront and beach. In time, a trail may be built heading uphill and connecting to the southwest corner of Gazzam Lake Park.

When you reach the intersection of Crystal Springs Rd. with Baker

Crystal Springs public beach donated by Bainbridge family

Hill Rd., you have walked .7 miles from the Point White dock. From here to the road end, there are very deep, wooded waterfront lots and steep forested hills above. The road gently curves as it heads north. The pavement ends at about 1.4 miles from the dock, but the road continues another .7 mile downhill, dead-ending at a private driveway. Turn around here and walk back.

For the ambitious in search of a little aerobic exercise and not concerned about walking alongside heavy traffic, a much more strenuous loop walk can be taken by forging up Baker Hill Rd. from Crystal Springs Rd. Follow it to Lynwood Center Rd., then right to Lynwood Center and back to the car along Point White Drive. Walking along Point White Drive between Lynwood Center and Point White is not recommended because of the narrow road without shoulders and the amount of traffic. However, it is a scenic walk along the shores of Rich Passage and Point White.

Eagledale Loops/Rockaway Beach Loop

Eagledale basic road loop 2.9 miles, light to moderate traffic.
Lots of options for shorter and longer walks.
Rockaway Beach Loop, 5 miles, light to moderate traffic.
Moderately strenuous, about as much up and down as one finds on Bainbridge.

THERE ARE A NUMBER OF LOOPS in the Eagledale area along mostly quiet roads that will keep walkers occupied for many separate trips. The basic loop takes one through "old Bainbridge," essentially rural with small farming here and there. It has the feel of the late 50's on Bainbridge for the most part, with lots of green open space, plenty of wetlands, old trees, smaller homes, sheep, horses, a chicken here and there and some dogs wandering on their own.

The basic loop begins at the corner of McDonald and Eagle Harbor Drive. Park on the north shoulder of the road. (If there is no room, park at Eagledale Park, or Joel Pritchard Park and use the map). Walk up McDonald and soon pass on your right a small farm meadow with treed hills, a miniature of such areas in Montana. (Use your imagination!) The road is named for Malcolm McDonald. McDonald was a leading citizen of the "Southside" in the 1880's, as Eagledale was known before it was named in a contest, the winner of which won cufflinks valued at $2.50. One of the major landowners in Kitsap County, he established the McDonald "ranch" with a large house, extensive barns, and many acres under cultivation.

At the intersection with Old Mill Rd., turn left. On your right is land owned by Islandwood, an outdoor learning center. There is public access to the Center on a scheduled and controlled basis. Continue on Old Mill to the intersection with Taylor Rd./Blakely Hill Rd., passing New Sweden Rd. along the way. Follow Taylor back to Eagle Harbor Drive and walk back uphill to the start point to complete the loop.

The basic loop is 2.9 miles and there is moderate traffic on Eagle Harbor Drive along with a bit of uphill walking. The loop can be shortened to 2.3 miles by taking New Sweden Rd., with its historic homes, many built by Scandinavians employed at Port Blakely. New Sweden Rd. and Taylor Ave are located on parts of the path of the first foot-trails of white settlers in the area, passing from Port Blakely over the hill.

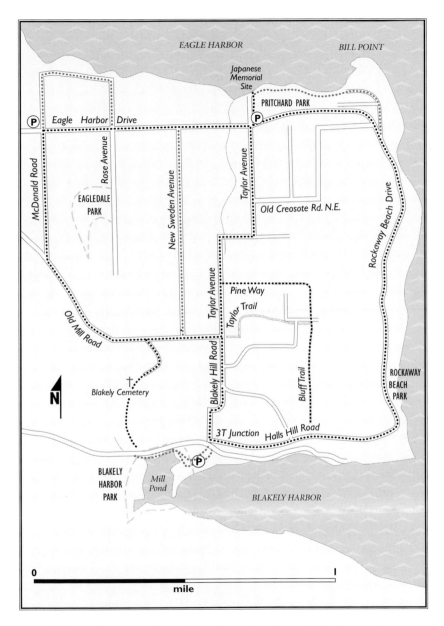

The basic loop can also be lengthened to about 4 miles by turning onto Old Creosote Rd. off Taylor Rd. and following it to its junction with Eagle Harbor Dr., then back to the car. Walkers with a bit of extra time will extend the walk by crossing Eagle Harbor Dr. and entering the Japanese Memorial Site and Joel Pritchard Park.

One other loop, Rose Loop, adds yet another mile to any of these walks, with great views of Eagle Harbor and an old neighborhood.

Any of these routes provides a real vista of Puget Sound, Seattle, the entrance to Eagle Harbor and Wing Point but there can be a lot of traffic along Eagle Harbor Drive.

For the more ambitious walker, seeking the longest possible road loop in the Eagledale area, from Eagledale, begin by walking up McDonald Rd. At the junction of Old Mill and Taylor/Blakely Hill Rd., turn onto Blakely Hill Road, following it sharply downhill to Three T junction. From here, explore Blakely Harbor, the mill pond, causeway and Blakely Harbor Park. Then head back up to Three T and travel right on Halls Hill Rd. uphill and then down, curving north with big vistas to the Sound, near shore rocks and lots of birds at times. To the east is Blakely Rock. Once underwater, an enormous earthquake about 1000 years ago lifted it 23 feet, forming an islet with a white crushed shell beach visible at low tide. Stop at the Rockaway Beach site acquired with Open Space funds. This small waterfront park is remarkable at a very low tide and scenic anytime. Continue to walk for nearly a mile on flat Rockaway Beach Dr., with close views of the Sound all the way. Use caution walking here as the road is narrow, cars sometimes travel fast, and pedestrians are few. Rockaway Dr. bends uphill and becomes Eagle Harbor Drive as it travels up, down, and up again to where you parked, passing two ravines in their natural state and the old Eagledale neighborhood.

One particularly notable place along the way is the Taylor Rd. area near the shore of Eagle Harbor. Mike Taylor was the first homesteader on Taylor Ave, homesteading 160 acres and establishing a logging camp nearby in 1875. Taylor Creek, a.k.a. Whiskey Creek, flows into Eagle Harbor. There are ongoing efforts to return salmon to the stream and if successful, visitors may be able to see salmon swimming upstream in the deep ravine to spawn in the fall.

If you take Taylor Rd. downhill toward the bay, you will reach the location of the dock from which Americans of Japanese ancestry were taken to be relocated in internment camps during World War II. The site is a National Historic Landmark. There is a memorial planned to commemo-

A little bit of Montana in Eagledale

rate this spot, as it has special significance to people everywhere, particularly those living on Bainbridge. At the time, the publishers of the Bainbridge Review wrote editorials condemning the relocation and internment. Bainbridge had a substantial population of Japanese-Americans who were interned and returned home to live on the Island.

The road end, in addition to its historic significance, adjoins the old Wyckoff creosote plant, a Superfund site. The entire site has been purchased by the City of Bainbridge and is named Joel Pritchard Park. The fenced point extending into Eagle Harbor is off-limits until the EPA finishes its cleanup remedy and the City determines what public use may be allowed on that portion of the park. Approximately half the site has been cleaned up and is open to public use. This public area includes a long stretch of sandy beach. Upon opening, it immediately became a popular spot for islanders. Eventually, walkers will be able to enter the park from the road which presently extends downhill to the point from Eagle Harbor Dr. at the east end of the site. The site is surely one of the finest locations for a park in all of Puget Sound, with views of Mt. Baker, the Cascade Mountains, Mt. Rainier, Seattle and the Olympic Mountains.

Blakely Harbor

Loop up Bluff Trail, Taylor Trail and back to Blakely Harbor Park

2.5 miles.

WITH THE ACQUISITION OF BLAKELY HARBOR PARK, Bainbridge walkers can take a variety of fine walks near the harbor. The park is at the head of the bay, which once supported a thriving lumber mill town and shipyard. Port Blakely Mill was visited by President Rutherford B. Hayes, who incidentally, was not invited to visit Port Madison, because the superintendent of the Port Madison mill company was a Democrat. The harbor was the main auto ferry link to Seattle from 1923 to 1937, when it was eliminated as a ferry terminal and all ferry service was consolidated to two landing sites in Eagle Harbor.

A new trail system has been built, extending from near Fort Ward State Park to Blakely Harbor Park, with plans to continue the trail and a

Blakely Harbor

walking route all the way from the parking area at Fort Ward State Park to Joel Pritchard Park. The existing trails travel primarily through wooded buffers in the newly developed Blakely Harbor area, crossing roads here and there. Islandwood, an outdoor learning center, has built a trail which crosses Blakely Ave to connect Blakely Harbor Park to Blakely Cemetery and Old Mill Road, so there will be lots of options for walks radiating from this new waterfront park.

From the park, head up Halls Hill Road .4 mile (there are plans for a trail along this stretch of road) to the Bluff Trail, found on the north side of Halls Hill Rd. at its intersection with Rockaway Bluff Dr. N.E. If you don't see it, walk up Rockaway Bluff Dr. N.E. and look for it on your left, near the small ponds. The trail travels north to a junction with the Taylor Trail, which is found across Barkentine Rd. Follow the trail as it continues north and then heads west onto Pine Way, eventually intersecting Taylor Rd. Walk south down Taylor and then down Blakely Hill Rd. back to Blakely Harbor Park. (There are plans for a trail alongside Blakely Hill Rd.)

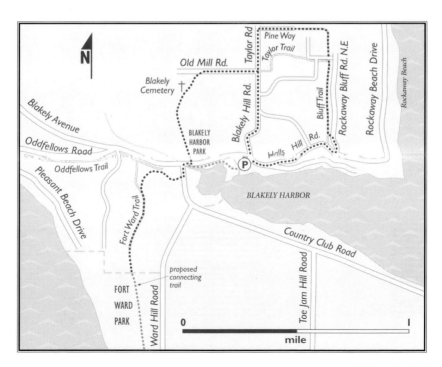

Old causeway in Blakely Harbor Park

Other options include the Oddfellows Trail, which begins opposite the park to the west across Country Club Road and the Blakely to Fort Ward trail beginning across Country Club Rd.

Flower gazing at Blakely Harbor Park

Fort Ward State Park Trails

Short loop inside Fort Ward State Park 2 miles.
To the end of South Beach and back, 4 miles, light traffic.
Up and over Toe Jam Hill Rd., 6.4, long and very steep up Toe Jam Hill.

POPULAR FORT WARD STATE PARK has a nice loop walk of slightly more than 2 miles, beginning at the parking lot just inside the park gate or at the parking lot next to the boat launch. The walk takes you along the interior park road, which is gated to cars. Pass between a stately row of maples arching over the road, walking just past the smaller Park Ranger's house and head toward the beach along a path through the blackberries and alders. The path takes you along the shoreline

Shoreline trail at Fort Ward State Park

and comes out at the east border of the park. From here, one can head back to the park road and then shortly, a spur road heads uphill into the forest, curving left toward the top and eventually into the upper parking lot. A trail heads west from the north end of the parking lot through the woods and back to the park road and your vehicle.

The park includes 137 acres of huge trees and about a mile of mostly rocky but very scenic beach. In the fall, walk along the trails and shuffle through the yellow, red and brown leaves from big leaf maple trees. There are mature western red cedar, Douglas fir, Pacific madrona, western hemlock and along the beach there are groves of

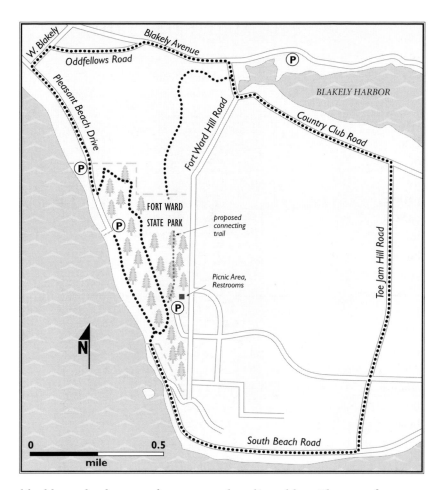

blackberry bushes, nootka roses, and sapling alder. There are frequent
ly bald eagles in the tree tops or in the sky overhead, cormorants
perched on the pilings in front of the park, and kinglets and wrens in
the brush along the sunny path near the water.

Named in honor of Colonel George H. Ward, who was wounded at
Gettysburg in 1863, the Fort was first a coast artillery and mine station
with battlements. It was built in 1900 along with others at Fort Worden,
Fort Flagler and Fort Casey to protect the Puget Sound Naval Shipyard
at Bremerton. Three eight-inch disappearing cannons were mounted in
hilltop batteries. Smaller gun batteries were on the beach. When World
War I broke out in Europe and the guns were needed in France, the Fort

Ward guns were taken out for shipment to Europe. By 1923, it was abandoned as a fort. It was subsequently used as a children's health and recreational camp for the State Dept. of Public Welfare during the Great Depression and as a top-secret naval radio station during World War II and the Cold War.

You can bring in picnic and barbecue makings and have a family outing along the shore at the picnic area or you can come in by kayak and stay overnight at the Marine Park campground just up from the beach. Expect big sky and sunshine at this park, if there is any chance to find it on Bainbridge. The park is located on the southwest side of the island, with spectacular views of the Olympic Mountains, Rich Passage, and the mainland beyond.

There are any number of possible extensions to the park loop walk. Continue out of the park on the east end, briefly along a waterfront residential street with great views, past the aquaculture dock and along South Beach Rd. to its intersection with Toe Jam Hill Rd., a total of another mile one way. Nearly the entire mile is next to the water and has very light vehicle traffic. From fall through spring, sea lions lounge away on the red buoy marking Bainbridge Reef, flopping on and off, arfing at regular intervals. By the time you get to Toe Jam Hill Rd. on a clear day you've had a great view of the Olympics, Mount Rainier and part of the Cascades. To the south is Blake Island, said to possibly be the birthplace of Chief Sealth, the paramount chief in the region. The diminutive resident deer are probably descendants of deer which the Native Americans hunted there. From South Beach Rd., one can visualize the canoes traveling back and forth between Restoration Point and Blake Island.

If you return on South Beach Rd., you've gone 4 miles. You can go 4.5 miles by heading up the old stairs off South Beach Rd. just before it meets Fort Ward Hill Rd. or by turning up Fort Ward Hill Rd. on your way back to the Park, continuing uphill to the intersection with an entrance road which leads to the upper parking lot at Fort Ward State Park. Enter the trail at the north edge of the parking lot, follow it through the upper park and eventually down to your car.

For a real day's walk, from the east end of South Beach Rd., head up very steep Toe Jam Hill, pausing to catch your breath while you think

Rich Passage

about people biking up Toe Jam Hill in the annual marathon, over the top and down to Country Club Road, 1.2 miles. Turn left and walk Country Club Road to Blakely Avenue, where you can visit Blakely Harbor Park. Head left .3 miles to Oddfellows Road, or walk the new Oddfellows trail through the woods to the same point. Turn onto Oddfellows, then south toward the water on W. Blakely Ave to Pleasant Beach Rd. and .5 mile back to the car, a grand total of 6.4 miles, all left turns. This route takes you by several historic homes in the West Blakely neighborhood, many of which were built by Scandinavians during Port Blakely's heyday as a mill and shipbuilding town. Alternatives include using Fort Ward Hill Rd. to shorten it up a bit, or taking Oddfellows Rd. all the way to Pleasant Beach Road, lengthening the walk to at least 7 miles. Mathematically, there are too many combinations to calculate, not to mention beginning at various points and alternating the direction of travel. It is remarkable how different the same walk will look if the route is reversed.

Fort Ward State Park to Joel Pritchard Park

Approximate length 4.2 miles.

WHEN ALL THE PROPOSED LINKS ARE COMPLETED, one will be able to walk from the shores of Rich Passage to the beach at Joel Pritchard Park on Eagle Harbor, a 4.2 mile trip, taking the shortest route. This walk includes about 1 mile on relatively quiet roads, but the great majority is on trails. There are plenty of side trips for ambitious travelers, as one can easily see by examining the maps that go with the Eagledale/-Rockaway Beach, Blakely Harbor, and Fort Ward walks. One could spend a full day exploring the area between these two public beaches.

Quiet pond on Fort Ward to Pritchard Park trail

Unless you want to make a long round-trip out of this walk, arrange to be dropped off and picked up or park at either Fort Ward or Joel Pritchard Park and leave another car at the opposite end.

Starting at Fort Ward, take the trail just north of the main waterfront parking lot uphill into the forest. At some point along this trail, it is proposed that there will be a trail heading off to the left. It will shortly exit Fort Ward, pass well below the sewage treatment plant, and head downhill on the fine trail built by developer Kelly Samson. At one point, this trail crosses a small road. Look for the next segment of the trial across the road, slightly off to your right. The trail then continues downhill, crossing the unmarked northern boundary of the western section of Blakely Harbor Park, passing a small pond and heading to the right, eventually

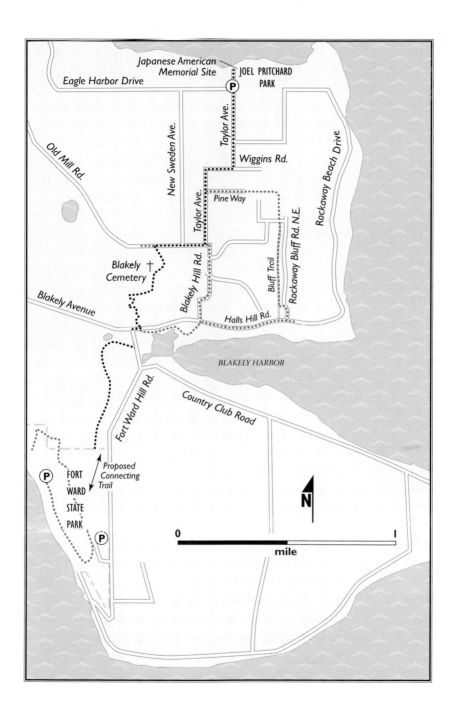

Japanese American
Memorial Site
JOEL PRITCHARD
PARK
Eagle Harbor Drive
P

New Sweden Ave.

Taylor Ave.

Old Mill Rd.

Wiggins Rd.

Taylor Ave.

Pine Way

Rockaway Beach Drive

Blakely Cemetery †

Blakely Hill Rd.

Bluff Trail

Rockaway Bluff Rd. N.E.

Blakely Avenue

Halls Hill Rd.

BLAKELY HARBOR

Fort Ward Hill Rd.

Country Club Road

P
FORT
WARD
STATE
PARK

Proposed
Connecting
Trail

P

N

0   1
mile

Eagle Harbor view from Pritchard Park beach

coming out at Country Club Rd. East across the road is a meadow portion of Blakely Harbor Park. Eventually, a trail will be built beginning directly across Country Club Rd. but until then, you must turn left and walk down the shoulder of the paved road until reaching the intersection with Blakely Ave. Turn right and there are two options. One, via the Bluff Trail, is described in the Blakely Harbor Park section of this book. A second option is to find the trail heading uphill on the left side of the road, approximately 100' east of the intersection of Country Club Rd. and Blakely Ave. You can take this trail uphill eventually passing next to the Blakely Cemetery, and out onto Old Mill Rd. Head right until reaching Taylor Ave /Blakely Hill Rd. Straight ahead, there is a marker leading to the Bluff and Taylor trail. (See Blakely Harbor map.) Follow the trail to its exit back out onto Taylor Rd.

Getting from Taylor Rd. to Joel Pritchard Park is straightforward. Taylor is a pleasant street to walk and you can continue across Eagle Harbor Dr., down to the shore of the harbor, the Japanese Memorial and Pritchard Park.

Bainbridge Road Ends

THE MANY PUBLIC ROAD ENDS LEADING TO BEACHES and bays on the island provide special opportunities for walkers on Bainbridge. The public can walk onto the beach at any of the public road ends described in this book, assuming that access is physically possible, i.e., it doesn't require dropping over a cliff or fighting through 100' of solid blackberry bushes. Some are difficult to find and Island committees have been working on establishing signage and continued access to many of these sites. Once on the beach, you may be trespassing if you wander outside the road right of way, unless you are adjacent to publicly owned shorelines or are walking below the mean low-tide line, generally on a minus tide. As Harvey Manning says in his books, "Be courteous. You don't want to have to hike with a lawyer."

Bainbridge residents are generally very tolerant of beach walkers but we cannot advise you to trespass under any circumstances.

One of Bainbridge Island's many road ends

SOURCES:

Kitsap County – A History. Kitsap Co. Historical Society, 1977

Streams of Bainbridge Island: Names, History, Folklore & Culture –
    Gerald Elfendahl 1996

Blakely Harbor Inventory & Report – Bainbridge Island Harbor
    Management Plan 1997

Bainbridge Island Park and Recreation District Comprehensive Plan 1996.

Bainbridge through Bifocals: Elsie Frankland Marriott – Gateway
    Printing, Seattle 1941

A History of Bainbridge Island – Katy Warner   1968

Washington: A Guide to the Evergreen State: WPA Writers Project –
    Binford & Morts, Portland Or. 1941

The Bloedel Reserve: Gardens in the Forest – Lawrence Kreisman
    Published by the Arbor Fund 1988

ACKNOWLEDGEMENTS.

David and Cindy Harrison, Ron Williamson, Martha Brouwer, Kay
Jensen, Reed Hansen, Gerry Elfendahl